Chronicle of Childhood

Fiona Reynoldson

This is a reference book. You can use it to find out about how the rich and poor lived and what their family life was like and how they were educated in the different periods in history.

Contents

Using the Chronicle	2
Romans (43–410)	4
Anglo-Saxons (c. 400–1066)	6
Vikings (c. 793–1066)	8
Normans (1066–1250)	10
Late Middle Ages (c. 1250–1485)	12
Tudors (1485–1603)	14
Stuarts (1603–1714)	16
1700s (1700–1800)	18
Early 1800s (1800–c. 1830)	20
Early Victorian Times (c. 1830–1870)	22
Late Victorian Times (1870–1901)	24
Early 1900s (1901–c. 1930)	26
Mid 1900s (c. 1930–1970)	28
Glossary	30
Further Information	32
Index	33

USING THE CHRONICLE

How the Chronicles are organised

The Chronicles are organised into parts. This is because history is easier to understand if we divide it into parts called **periods**. These periods are sections of time in history.

This book has been organised into 13 periods. Each period has a starting date and an ending date. Of course, we cannot always say exactly when one period ends and another starts, so the dates are just a guide.

The choice of periods

Each of the Chronicles in the Longman Book Project cover the same 13 periods of history. To help you remember the periods, there is a special memorable event for each one shown in the top right hand corner.

Subheadings

On each page there are a number of headings and subheadings. The subheadings are the same for each period. This helps you to compare facts about children from one period with facts about children from another period.

The timeline

On the bottom of each page there is a timeline. The timeline stretches from Roman times to the present day. There was plenty of history **before** Roman times but it is not covered in this book.

AD | 1500

How to use the book for research

You can use the Chronicle to compare information from one period with another. For instance, you might want to compare home and family life in one period with home and family life in another. If this is all you need to know, you can just read the information under these subheadings and ignore the rest of the writing.

How to use the Chronicles to cross-reference

You might want to research using more than one of the Chronicles in the Longman Book Project. You can easily do this, because each Chronicle covers the same periods in history. You can therefore compare the information in one Chronicle with that in another.

THE ROMANS

Rich children

How they lived

Rich boys learnt to fight, to ride horses, and to study history, philosophy, geometry, music, astronomy and geography. Rich Romans dressed in fine clothes and had plenty of slaves to do the housework, cooking and farming.

Reading, writing and education

Rich Roman children started school at about six years old, but most of them left at the age of eleven years. They learnt the alphabet first and then they learnt how to read. They also learnt to write by scratching letters on a wax covered wooden board.

Some rich boys went on to secondary school, or, like the emperor's son, had teachers who came to their homes.

Home and family life

Rich children in Roman times lived in large houses. They had servants or slaves to do the housework.

A Roman Emperor and his family. When the boy on the right grew up and became Emperor, he murdered his brother and then scratched his brother's face out of the picture.

AD 01   AD 500

Poor children – slaves

How they lived

Many of the poor people in Roman times were slaves. Slaves were people who were owned by the rich. They earned no money and had no rights. When the Romans conquered a new country, they made all their prisoners, including children, into slaves. They sold the women, children and men to Roman citizens.

Slaves did all sorts of different work. Some young slaves might be trained to be teachers. Other slaves worked in kitchens, on farms or in mines deep underground.

Reading, writing and education

Most poor children never learnt to read or write. However, some clever boy slaves who belonged to kind Romans were sent to school with the families' own children. If they did well, they might help to run their owners' shops or factories. They might even become teachers, musicians or librarians.

Home and family life

A child sold into slavery might never see his family again after the sale. The Roman citizens who owned him became his family. If they were kind, he had a happy time. Later, when he was older, the rich family might give him his freedom as a present. However, many slaves were badly treated and beaten, and had a miserable life.

A statue of a Roman slave boy.

Rich children

How they lived

Many of the Anglo-Saxons became Christians, and they set up monasteries. Both boys and girls from rich families were educated by the monks and nuns in the monasteries. Some boys stayed in the monasteries to become monks. Some boys left the monasteries and went home to marry and to run households of their own.

When the girls grew up, they usually went back to their families, and they often married kings or noblemen.

Reading, writing and education

The monasteries ran the only schools of the time, so some rich children went to school in monasteries. Some girls as well as the boys were taught to read and write.

Home and family life

In Anglo-Saxon times women could own their own land or homes. Rich girls were often well educated, and many kings listened to the advice of their wives. They also gave their wives a lot of responsibility: they left them to look after the kingdoms when they were away. If the king died before his son was old enough to rule, the queen would rule until the boy was grown up.

A rich boy having his hair cut ➦

AD 01   AD 500

Poor children – peasants

How they lived

Life was very different for the poor. Poor people had to work very hard. Most children lived with their families in mud cottages that had only one room. They worked with their parents from the moment they were old enough to toddle. The girls collected firewood, did some of the cooking, herded animals, and helped to look after the younger children. The boys helped on the farm.

Reading, writing and education

No one saw the need for children from peasant families to learn to read and write. Books were very expensive.

Home and family life

Children were very important to Anglo-Saxon peasants. They needed to have children to work on their farms and to look after them in their old age. They often had many children, but usually several of them died when they were young.

 An Anglo-Saxon drawing showing a child being bathed.

VIKINGS *circa 793–1066*

Rich children

How they lived

The Vikings were raiders and traders who came from Scandinavia. They went to raid countries like Britain. They left the women and children to run the farms.

Some Viking men decided to settle in Britain. So they put their families in their ships, as well as all the animals they could fit in, and they set sail for the north east coast of Britain. The rich Vikings were the leaders and their children ate better food than the others, and they wore better clothes.

Reading, writing and education

Reading and writing were not important for Viking boys and girls. Some Vikings lived by sailing across the seas to other countries to raid and steal. They did not need the skills of reading and writing.

Home and family life

Although the Vikings were known for their raiding, back home in Scandinavia they lived as farmers most of the time. All summer the women ran the farms on the low land on the shores of the fiords. Often the boys took the cows up into the mountains to graze on the summer grass, while the girls stayed with their mothers to look after the crops and the smaller animals. When the Vikings settled in Britain, many became farmers.

◄ Figures from a Viking chess set.

AD 01   AD 500

AD 793 – The first Viking raid on Britain.

Poor children – Viking traders

How they lived

Ordinary children lived in almost the same way as rich children. The boys learnt to fight, and the girls to sew. However, poorer children lived in simple wooden huts and wore rough clothes. They knew that they would grow up to live the same sort of lives as their parents, and that they would have to obey their rich leaders.

Home and family life

The Vikings lived in wooden houses with only one room. There were low beds around the walls that could be used as seats. The fire was in the centre, and it was used for cooking and for warmth. Children lay in bed at night listening to the stories sung and told by the grown ups as they sat around the fire.

Reading, writing and education

Many of the Vikings who settled in the north east of England lived by trading things like furs and food. The children grew up helping in the house and loading the ships. Most of them did not learn to read and write – except perhaps for a few words, so that they could write down what they had bought and sold.

↑ A model of a Viking woman weaving cloth with her children.

NORMANS 1066–1250

Rich children

How they lived

Norman boys were brought up to fight. At eight years old boys were sent away from their own homes to live in the houses of more important knights. There they learnt to look after horses, armour and weapons. When they were older, they practised leaping on to their horses, wearing their chain mail armour.

Girls stayed at home and learnt how to run a household.

Reading, writing and education

Some rich Normans wanted their sons to learn to read and write. Monks or priests sometimes taught them. If a rich Norman had many sons, he trained some to be soldiers and sometimes he sent some to monasteries to become monks. There they learnt to read and write, and perhaps to copy some of the beautiful books that were made in the monasteries.

Home and family life

Boys did not spend much time with their families after the age of eight. Girls were taught by their mothers, aunts and women servants. Sometimes well-educated women taught their daughters to read or sent them to convents (run by nuns) to learn reading and writing, but in those days a girl's job was to prepare to be a wife and mother.

AD 1066 – The Normans won the Battle of Hastings.

Poor children – peasants

How they lived

Peasants were farmers who had only a small amount of land. They grew a few crops and kept some animals. Their life was very hard. Peasant girls and boys lived in huts with only one or two rooms. The huts were made using wattle and daub, twigs smeared with mud, and had thatched roofs.

The children helped their parents in the fields, often working ten hours a day.

Reading, writing and education

Poor children had very little education. Only merchants and shopkeepers taught their children a little reading, writing and adding up.

Home and family life

Families were not very large, because many children died before the age of five. There were many illnesses then, including the bubonic plague which killed thousands of people in late Norman times and in the Middle Ages.

◂◂ This scene from the Bayeux tapestry, which was begun in 1077, shows a woman and child being burnt out of their home.

MIDDLE AGES

Rich children

How they lived

As always in history, having babies was a woman's main job. Therefore rich girls were brought up to marry rich men and have children. From Norman times onwards, men owned all the land and money. They wanted to have sons so that they could pass their land and money on to them. It was important that when a girl married, she had sons. Most girls were only important because they could become wives and mothers of rich men, and so make the whole family richer.

Reading, writing and education

Rich children did have some lessons in the late middle ages. Girls were taught embroidery, singing and dancing.

Boys were taught to read and write and ride a horse.

Home and family life

The homes of rich children were often made of stone. The homes were lit with candles and heated by fires.

Usually children did not have a choice about whom they married.

The birth of a baby in a rich family

AD 01   AD 500

Poor children – farmers

How they lived

Farmers' daughters were brought up to work hard on the farm. The girls gathered wood for fires, looked after animals, and learnt to cook in cauldrons over open fires in the centre of the house. They learnt to preserve food for the hard times in winter, and they helped to look after the younger children. The boys helped on the farm too.

Reading, writing and education

In the late Middle Ages, it was very unlikely that a farmer's child would learn to read and write.

Home and family life

Most farms were run by families. Everyone worked to grow enough food for the family to eat. The girls and boys helped.

A woman and baby in a house. In the late Middle Ages there was no glass in the windows.

Rich children

How they lived

Rich children were dressed like small grown ups. This was because grown ups did not think children were very important. They just wanted them to grow up and be useful.

Some rich children were brought up to be courtiers. A courtier lived at the king or queen's court and the men often helped to govern the country.

Reading, writing and education

This was a time in history when more and more of the sons of rich people learnt to read and write. This was partly because there was more trading and boys needed to learn to keep accounts if they were going to be merchants when they grew up. The monasteries were closed down by Henry VIII, but more schools were opened. They were only for boys. Some rich girls were well educated too but they were mainly taught at home.

Home and family life

Children wore clothes that were exactly like grown up clothes. They wore stiff ruffs around their necks. The girls wore long dresses, and the boys wore doublets and hose – thick stockings that were held up by laces which tied them on to the underclothes. Children from rich families often spent a lot of time with servants, and they did not see much of their mothers and fathers.

◄ The explorer Sir Walter Raleigh and his son.

AD 01   AD 500

Poor children – farmers

How they lived

There were many farms in Tudor times. Boys and girls worked on the family farm. They would look after the animals and help with the harvest.

Reading, writing and education

We do not know how many ordinary children learnt to read and write. By Tudor times, some children were taught by their parents, or by the vicar, or at a little village school. They probably could not read very well, because they left school at about eight years old.

Home and family life

Many poor children lived in one room heated by a fire in the middle of the room. The huts had thatched roofs but very few had windows.

The whole family helped on the farm. The sons learnt to read and write so they could write down how much money their family made at market.

Tudor farmers ploughing a field and planting seeds.

STUARTS 1603–1714

Rich children

How they lived

Rich children were brought up to help run the house and land where the family lived. Rich boys and girls were dressed in beautiful clothes made from silk and lace. Their clothes were just like smaller versions of adults' clothes.

Reading, writing and education

By Stuart times rich children were taught to read and write by teachers who came to live in the palace or great house. The boys, and sometimes the girls, learnt French, history, and a few other subjects.

Home and family life

Rich children were expected to marry someone chosen by their parents. Kings made sure that their sons married princesses. Royal children often had foreign mothers or foreign princesses in the family.

 Rich children in Stuart times.

AD 1666 – The Great Fire of London.

Poor children – beggars

How they lived

All through history, some people have always been very poor. Often this was because they were ill or crippled. In Stuart times there were many beggars. Some beggars tried to make a real job of begging. They brought their children up to beg. Occasionally this meant injuring their own children. The children would then be expected to show their injuries, and they would hope that passers-by would feel sorry for them and give them money.

Often women with young children or crippled people really needed to beg – otherwise they would starve to death.

Reading, writing and education

Beggars had neither the money to pay a teacher, nor the need to learn to read and write.

Home and family life

Whether rich or poor, children were part of the family group. They were fed and looked after, but in return they had to work. A beggar child had to beg and to earn money for the whole family.

A poor family in Stuart times.

1700s 1700–1800

Rich children

How they lived

Boys were brought up to run the house when their fathers died. Girls were brought up to marry and to leave home.

As you can see from the painting children were dressed like adults from an early age.

Reading, writing and education

Boys from rich families were taught by a teacher at home. Some rich boys went on to university.

The girls were taught to read and write at home. They learnt some music and painting, and perhaps some French and other subjects. However, in most families their studying was much less serious than that of the boys.

Home and family life

Although many children died young from diseases like smallpox, children from rich families had a better chance of living than children from poorer families. Rich children had better food, and they lived in dry houses.

 Rich children in the 1700s.

AD 01   AD 500

AD 1776 – The Americans declare their independence from Britain.

Poor children – street sellers

How they lived

The children often did the same jobs as their parents did. In the 1700s, many things were sold in the streets. Women, children and men sold fruit, rabbits, hot pies, gingerbread, fish, muffins, milk, and even buckets of water. Children worked with their parents, carrying baskets and shouting out what was for sale.

Reading, writing and education

Most poor children had no need to learn to read and write, although some were able to write their own name.

Home and family life

Often whole families worked together. They all took home the money they earned, to help the family.

In the 1700s, many people died young, and children were often left as orphans. They had nobody to look after them, so they had to look after themselves.

A milk maid and other street sellers.

Rich children

How they lived

Rich children did not have to work in the way poor children did. The girls were expected to marry rich men and to live in large houses with servants to cook and clean for them. As so often in history, a girl's life depended on the man she married. Parents often chose husbands for their daughters. Good parents did not make a daughter marry someone she did not like.

Reading, writing and education

Some rich girls were well educated. They had a teacher or governess who lived in the house. They learnt to read and write, and they also learnt several languages, such as French and Italian. They learnt some music and art as well.

Home and family life

Rich families often went out riding together for fun. The children often shared a small pony, and both the boys and the girls might go out hunting with their parents or with a groom to look after them. They played games, read, painted, went for walks, and visited friends.

Children playing battledore (now called badminton).

AD 01   AD 500

Poor children – labourers

How they lived

Poor children had to work as soon as they were able to. Often they did the same jobs as their parents. Some small children worked as bird scarers. They spent the day in the fields waving rattles to keep the crows away from the corn. Knitting was a common job in some places. All knitting in those days was done by hand, not by machine, and whole families knitted gloves, socks, scarves, shawls, and so on.

Reading, writing and education

Poor children might not go to school at all. However, some parents would try to find a few pennies a week to send their children to a little village school, so they could learn some reading and writing. Religious parents might want their children to be able to read the Bible a little.

Home and family life

Families were large. However, in the early 1800s many people died of disease. The average length of life for a poor person in a town was about 20 years (Nowadays the average length of life is about 70 years).

Families lived in small cottages that had only one or two rooms.

Many families made a living out of knitting.

Rich children

How they lived

As in other periods in history there was a big difference in the life styles of the rich and the poor. Rich children did not have to work, because they had lots of money. They grew up to spend money and to live in big houses.

Reading, writing and education

Rich children had teachers at home when they were young. Later the boys were sent away to school. By mid Victorian times rich people sent their sons to schools which are now famous like Eton, Harrow, Rugby and Winchester. The boys lived in the schools as boarders. They learnt Latin, Greek, history and mathematics, but very little science or geography.

Home and family life

When rich children were very young, they were looked after by special nurses for children, called nannies. They lived in their own part of the house, called the nursery. The boys were often sent away to their first schools at the age of seven or eight years, and came home only for the holidays. Most girls stayed at home and were taught by governesses, but some went to boarding or day schools.

At the race course a rich boy has lost all his money.

AD 01   AD 500

Poor children – labourers

How they lived

Ordinary children worked from when they were young. They usually worked at whatever their parents worked at.

Reading, writing and education

By mid-Victorian times many children from poor families did go to school, although not usually for very long. Children who worked in the cotton mills went to school for an hour or two a day. The children of farm-workers went to the village school for a few years to learn to read and write a little.

Home and family life

Many new jobs were created in Victorian times. Some of these were jobs in factories or on the railways, but some were jobs in offices, writing letters. Many parents started to realise that their children might get better jobs if they could read and write. Families still lived in small cottages in the country or in single rooms in the cities, but many parents hoped that their children might live in better houses.

◂ At the centre of the picture a little girl is selling flowers to rich people in a carriage.

LATE VICTORIAN TIMES 1870–1901

Rich children

How they lived

Many rich children knew that they would never have to go out to work, because their parents had plenty of money. However, some children who came from rich families knew that they still had to get jobs. The boys might go into their fathers' businesses.

Reading, writing and education

If the boys were going to run businesses they had to be able to read and write and to keep accounts. They often went to local schools and then went into the business or shop. The sons of very rich businessmen went to public schools and perhaps to university.

Home and family life

Rich people spent a lot of time spending money. They had many servants, horses, clothes and big houses. The children often spent quite a lot of time with their nannies when they were young and with other servants when they were older. Their fathers were often busy running businesses and their mothers ran the household.

Two rich school boys in uniform.

AD 1870 – The beginning of free education for all children.

Poor children – factory workers

How they lived

Poor children's parents often worked in factories. Boys and girls were brought up to work in the same factories as their parents.

Reading, writing and education

From the 1880s all children had to go to school until they were eleven years old. Parents did not have to pay any fees. For the first time ever, all children had the chance to learn to read and write.

Home and family life

By late Victorian times most people, even poor people, were better off. Not so many children died when they were young because there was more food to eat. This meant that some families were very large. There was usually enough food, but there was often no money left over to buy shoes as well.

 Boys from Birmingham on an outing in 1888.

Rich children

How they lived

Girls from rich families were still expected to grow up and get married. But some girls were wanting something more from life. Some parents thought it was a good idea for girls to have careers. They sent their daughters to good schools, and encouraged them to work hard and do well. Other parents were horrified that rich girls might have careers. They insisted that their daughters should stay at home until they married rich husbands.

Reading, writing and education

All children had to go to school until they were eleven or twelve, or they had to have a teacher at home.

Some rich children went to school until the age of 18 and then on to university.

Home and family life

Many rich families had a lot of children. The children were often very strictly brought up. They often lived in a very large house, and they all had to do exactly what their father said. This included everything – from when they could use the bathroom to what jobs they were to go into when they left school!

A small boy in the early 1900s. Boys wore the same clothes as girls until they were about 5 years old.

Poor children – farmworkers

How they lived

In the early 1900s, several million men, women and children still worked in the country, on farms. The wages were not good and so children often had to work after school to help pay for food and clothes.

Reading, writing and education

Children had to go to school until they were 11 years old. Most schools only had one class for about 60 children of all ages but all children had the chance to learn to read and write.

Some people did not take school seriously. Mothers who went out to work sometimes kept daughters off school to look after younger children. Farmers sometimes insisted that boys should stay off school to work for them at harvest time.

Home and family life

Life was difficult for poor families. They often didn't have enough to eat. Their homes were not well built and were very small.

 A farm worker's cottage in 1900.

Rich children

How they lived

By the mid 1900s there were fewer very rich people (and also fewer very poor people). Most people belonged to the "middle classes". They might have a little or a lot of money but they almost all had to work to earn a living.

Parents knew that their children and grandchildren must be well-educated, because when they grew up, they would need to learn to be engineers or to work at new jobs running factories or shops.

Reading, writing and education

Rich children went to expensive schools, and they learnt to read and write with other rich children. They were expected to pass exams and to get qualifications. To get a good job a person had to pass exams.

Home and family life

In the mid-1900s families were much smaller than they had been in the early 1900s. Many parents only wanted to have one or two children. They wanted to spend more money on their children. Rich people did not have so many servants any more, and they found it hard work looking after their own children.

A rich schoolgirl travelling to see her parents who were living abroad in the 1930s.

Poor children

How they lived

For the first time in history, ordinary children had the chance to have good jobs when they grew up. Girls no longer had to get married. There were other jobs for them to do. Gradually between 1930 and 1970 more interesting jobs became open to women. Boys too had the chance to choose what sort of work they could do best. They did not just have to do what their fathers did. The biggest change for ordinary children was that they did not have to start work at the age of six or seven years. They went to school until they were fifteen years old (sixteen from 1972).

Reading, writing and education

In the 1940s the school leaving age went up to fifteen years of age. This meant that all children had the chance to learn a good deal and to study for examinations too. Schools were free, and some very good schools were built and run for ordinary children to go to.

Home and family life

Although most children live in warm houses with their parents, there are still some children who live on the streets of towns and cities.

 Children living on the streets in London.

GLOSSARY

Abbess — An abbess is a woman who is head of an abbey.

Armour — Armour is special clothing worn for protection. It was often made of metal.

Astronomy — Astronomy is the study of the stars and planets.

Bubonic plague — Bubonic plague is a deadly illness, with swellings (or buboes) in places such as the armpits.

Cauldron — A cauldron is a large cooking pot.

Chain mail armour — Chain mail armour was a certain type of armour, made from hundreds of rings of iron or steel.

Circa — Circa means about, or around. It is used when we are not sure about exact dates.

Citizens — Citizens are the people who live in a particular city or country.

The Civil War — The Civil War was the war between the Cavaliers (supporters of the king), and the Roundheads (the supporters of Parliament).

Conquered — Countries that have been conquered have been invaded and then ruled by the same invading country.

Convents — Convents are places where nuns live. They live their lives in the service of God.

Cotton mills — Cotton mills were factories where cotton thread and cloth were made.

Doublets — Doublets were close fitting jackets.

Embroidery	Embroidery is the sewing of patterns on to cloth.
Emperor	An emperor is someone who rules an empire, just as a king rules a country.
Empire	An empire is a lot of countries which are all controlled by one country.
Fiords	A fiord is a long, narrow inlet of the sea – Norway has many fiords.
Kingdoms	A kingdom is an area which is ruled by a king.
Merchant	A merchant is someone who buys and sells goods, such as wool and wine.
Monastery	A monastery is a building where monks live. They live their lives in the service of God.
Peasant	A peasant is a farmer with only a small amount of land.
Philosophy	Philosophy is the study of all knowledge.
Preserve	To preserve food is to stop it from going bad.
Ruffs	Ruffs were stiff frills which were worn around the neck.
Ruthless	Someone who is ruthless has no pity or compassion for anybody else.
Scandinavia	In Viking times Scandinavia was made up from Norway, Sweden, Denmark and Iceland.

FURTHER INFORMATION

It is often difficult to find out about children's lives in history.

One of the best ways is to look at old paintings and photographs and see what the children are doing in them.

Local museums and art galleries are useful.

Museums

Birmingham City Museum and Art Gallery has a large collection of paintings and a selection on local history.

Museum of Childhood, Bethnal Green, London.

Museum of Childhood, Edinburgh.